I0088512

Jumping Drawbridges in Technicolor

Mike James

∂

BLUE HORSE PRESS REDONDO BEACH, CALIFORNIA 2019

JUMPING DRAWBRIDGES
IN TECHNICOLOR

MIKE JAMES

Blue Horse Press
318 Avenue I # 760
Redondo Beach,
California   90277

Copyright © 2019 by Mike James
All rights reserved
Printed in the United States of America

Cover art: Jeffrey C. Alfier,
"Manasquan River Rail Bridge"

Editors: Jeffrey and Tobi Alfier
Blue Horse Press logo: Amy Lynn Hayes (1996)

ISBN 978-0-578-46581-4

No part of this book may be reproduced or transmitted in any form or by any means, electronic or mechanical, including photocopy, recording, or any information storage and retrieval system now known or to be invented, without permission in writing from the publisher, except by a reviewer who wishes to quote brief passages in connection with a review written for inclusion in a magazine, newspaper or broadcast.

FIRST EDITION © 2019

This and other Blue Horse Press Titles may be found at www.bluehorsepress.com

Acknowledgments

Some poems appeared, often in different versions, in the following magazines:

Front Range Review, Philadelphia Poet, As It Ought To Be, Philosophical Idiot, Trailer Park Quarterly, Good Works Review, Third Wednesday, Varnish, The Main Street Rag, Misfit, Laurel Review, Verse Virtual, Verse Wisconsin, Ted Ate America, The Artifact, Vox Populi, Heron Clan, Mojave River Review, Gasconade Review, and *Uppagus.*

"Everyone longs for bad reasons for most of their lives."

Jordan Rice

"Find another Eden, another apple tree
Somewhere, if you can."

James Baldwin

Contents

I.

My Wife's Shoes

Thankfully, my feet are small or her feet are large or both of us have feet slightly out of proportion to the rest of oh-so-very typical bodies. We don't *complete each other* in the way of puzzles, myths, and romantic movies. No, we are the near miss most couples are. But as for our shoes...they commingle happily in our closet and on our feet. She wears my flip flops. I wear her sandals. She looks formal and very British banker in my black wingtips. I clean room after room in her flats. And some nights we turn the radio to ballroom music and I pretend to be Fred Astaire, led by Ginger Rogers for a change, and dance in high heels in reverse.

Just Another Family Reunion

My sisters and I argue over who is the biggest disappointment. My parents say it's a tie. When we play cards we bet mistakes. I'll see your DUI and raise you a divorce. I'll add a divorce to yours and throw in a bankruptcy. This is how it is whenever we get together. Our kids play or else beat each other until their faces resemble bruised tomatoes. Our father sits on the couch and dreams of a better remote. In the kitchen our mother adds tears to the soup she's been cooking all these years.

Beyond The Land Of Misfit Toys

Drop that bucket into the memory well and it's never what
you wish. You pull up clown porn. (Yes, that's a thing.)
Shot glasses serve as telescopes to galaxies you'd rather not
see. Even one night stands, much heralded in the movies,
offer minimum relief. Every woman you end up with
wears heels or boots you desire more than her. You beg to
be her carpet, her footstool, her bath mat. If the question
is lust, the answer is confusion. You look at every closet
and hope for big locks. More than the butterfly you love
the butterfly tattoo.

That One Singer

Seems to know your life…How you lift yourself, just a little, from your seat when she reaches up past the ceiling, the roof, the trees, up near that first cloud to hit a high note…Or how you almost brace for a train to thunder by when she growls down and down with low ones…It's like she looked out the window, for no good reason, the night you got your first streetlight kiss…As if she knows how you got that knee scrape from belt buckle dodging at ten…

In Regards To Your Query

for Daniel Crocker

If I could be a super hero, I'd be Elvis. If you don't think
Elvis is a super hero, you weren't raised in the red
southern dirt of the early 1970's. Probably didn't have a
mother and grandmother who said, "Lord, that's a good
looking man" every time Elvis graced television's every
color.

If I were Elvis...the man...The King...I'd sing, perfectly,
in bad movies and, secretly, wish they were better. Beneath
stage lights, I'd drench towel after towel and still smell
fresh. Women would see my lips curl and my hips shake
and they would swoon and swoon. I'd escape to
Graceland, my not-at-all-secret-lair, and pace barefoot at
night across shag carpet until I could shock anyone who
came near.

The Story Of My Parents As A Shelf Of Books

Poor People. Snake Charmer's Daughter. Tough Guys
Don't Dance. Sometimes a Great Notion. Answered
Prayers. In Dreams Begin Responsibilities. On the Road.
A Tale of Two Cities. Post Office. A Confederacy of
Dunces. Sea Battles on Dry Land. Infinite Jest. Black
Spring. Pictures From an Institution. Recovery. Collected
Stories. Letting Go.

On Someone's Anniversary

For the sake of argument, let's have one. It's been a while.
At least a couple of hours since the last atomic blow up.
You think the world would be better with sprinkles. I
mostly disagree. Also, if I won the lottery, I'd invest in
umbrella stocks and unicorn farms. I'm a planner like that.
You'd spend it all on antique kitchen utensils and
misshapen power tools, on oil paintings of Karl Marx and
faux leather lampshades embroidered with the face of
Mayakovsky. You'd start calling our house an estate and
re-name it *In Memory of My Feelings*. That's just like you.
Plus, and I'm sure of this, your pockets would always
bulge with quarters and breath mints. And your belt would
be decorated with pet rocks in case you decided to take a
swim.

Wish Factory

Start out making a ham sandwich, end up trying to lick your elbow. Start out trying to lick your elbow, end up painting your nails. Start out painting your nails, end up in a large bubble bath with a stranger. Start out bathing joyfully with a stranger, end up making excuses for Christmas dinner. Start out making excuses for Christmas dinner, end up decorating the tree with hate notes and other handmade ornaments from throughout the year.

This Life

Yesterday a half-built mansion. Open to rain, raccoons, and a few young, stray vandals. Today a hunter's shack, cold in the woods, where shadows gather around a ghost fire. Tomorrow's foundation rocks scattered across a damp, distant field of knife-like weeds, grey blooming flowers.

Looking For Love In All The Wrong Places

Not in the instant coffee jar. Not in the breadbox, which is much too large. Not beneath the bed with the one white sock and the barely countable dust bunnies. Not outside, atop the paint-chipped concrete turtle. Not in the church pews. Not in the steeple. Not behind any peek-a-boo curtains on hot nights in late summer. Definitely not in the drug store. All the postcards there have statues of heroes who forgot love one moment after they turned to stone.

Jack's Personal Ad

Impoverished artist/scholar of some fifty-odd years.
Jagged. Feisty. Insistent on arcane myths. Large build, with
shapely paunch the size of two small turkey roasters side-
by-side. Gouty on misty days, plus Arbor Day and July 4th.
Fluent in Spanish, Esperanza, Parrot, and Seagull. Talent
for long conversations over black coffee. Also, can tie a
bow tie. In search of romance, friendship, communion
with angels, someone to waltz backwards with during
Sunday trips to either the zoo or the moon.

II.

Rebel, Rebel

for David Bowie

Once he took off his dress, he didn't know what to wear.
He tried walking around, naked as sunlight. Despite
summer days, that became quite drafty. And nothing held
in place. Appendages sagged, this way and that. So he put
on a blue suit, same color blue Candy Darling used for
lipstick. The color looked more natural romantic on her.
He wore the suit to walk the dog, shop for scarves, take
out the trash, and order delivery cheese pizza. Despite
adjustments from a sensible tailor, the suit was never a
perfect fit. In stilettos he no longer liked the click heels
made for his ears.

Edward, Oh Edward

Gave up dreaming because he could. Decided to cloud watch instead. He really wanted to go to Rome and cloud watch there. He heard Rome has the oldest clouds. Cloud watching is like coloring without crayons. When he was kid, he never had crayons. All he had was clouds and dreams and a pet monkey named Gilgamesh who walked with him when he took a walk and fed pigeons with him in the park. He loved Gilgamesh until he ran away to a circus. That's always the risk. Even his mother said that.

Wonderland

Nevertheless, Alice some rabbit holes are meant to be
covered otherwise populations in slow, faraway places,
down one way and near another, increase and increase
until those places are less roundly distant, less magically
hatted with their teacup wonder, no more special than any
chain store or any run of the mill garbage man out there
collecting his stars.

Oh Daddy, Give Me A Quarter For The Time Machine

I want to go to Berlin! Back before reunifications or walled up divisions, back before that screaming little man with his silly mustache. Yes, I want to go to the Weimar Republic and catch, just one, cabaret. See Marlene sulk sexy onto the stage in black top hat, tux (with white gloves, of course.) I want to see the scribblers making napkin notes for later. Hello, Walter Benjamin with your weak tea and indigestion. Good evening to you, Mr. Brecht, with your new girlfriend and old, out of tune guitar. Kurt Weill at the piano smoking his black, extra-long filter. Some unknown Sally at a barstool listening to other people's dreams.

Grace Jones

Never go backwards, darling. Let's make that clear. If you
have hair enough, toss it back. Paint your cheeks like the
family garden with whatever's near. Stick out the arrows of
your breasts to lead one way. Walk straight like a soldier or
crooked with a swish. Smile at all the secrets you wish to
possess.

Questions For Marilyn Monroe

How many years does sexy last? Feel free to be
approximate or specific.
How long did it take to hear Marilyn instead of Norma
Jean in your dreams?
Did you practice signing your name?
Pouting in the mirror?
Which of the Kennedy brothers did you prefer?
Was the kindest the smartest?
Was one better in bed?
Were you acting even then?
Was love a pose you thought you could hold?

Reading Sandburg's *Lincoln* While Getting A Pedicure

Though Egyptians painted their toenails centuries before
Cleopatra seduced her first Roman, Lincoln, probably,
never considered such a painterly act. What he knew of
tenderness and color stayed above his feet. No one ever
scrubbed away boot burnt, prairie dust from his giant toes.
He was never offered the choice of flavored bottled water
or even, yes, very sweet, very cheap white wine.

All we know is he preferred boots to sandals. We know
this from photographs. There are only a few photos of his
worn-down, broken smile. Not one photo of his bare feet,
desk propped to display gold or silver toe rings.

The Brownies Of Alice B. Toklas

Some women have small thin mustaches, pepper black, soft as a blanket worn to over-ripe thread. The mustache might be softer than the face it decorates, which might be all points and slopes. Descriptive enough? Gertrude says, description is not literature. If you only wish to see what others see you can only look at color photographs. Never at words. Even road signs read differently depending on where you are going, where you have been, if it is raining, and if the sun is shining through the rain. The sign might be on a street in Oakland, California, which always seems distant even if you are only one city over. As places go it is just as good as any other place, certainly no better.

The Guitar Lesson

after Balthus

She scraped her knees running to, what she knew, was her
last lesson. She never cried. Her body, half numb with
anticipation. Her teacher cleaned the blood away before
they started. Tenderly, dabbed each knee with a
handkerchief until only a plum's redness remained.

Knowing the lessons nearly finished, they said almost
nothing. Went right to the reason they were now together.

In her rush to her teacher, she almost forgot her guitar.

The Body

after a line by Jaime Shearn Coan

What is more present than the body? The sky is present in blue. The body's true scent is melancholy masked with soaps, deodorants, and perfumes. The body is present with yes. In sleep it follows the shape of the comma. In pain, it is a knotted period. Like commas, periods can be pauses. Temporary, like the body. A map of sacred graffiti in shades of blue.

III.

The Mime

His mother never quit talking. She couldn't sew a button or not burn toast or properly use a tissue on any tear, but she could talk. No telegraph silences. Just an electric hum, long as day.

So he wanted a quiet place. He found a box, with invisible walls. Crawled right in.

After a while, after silence became as empty as a shell and the sound of his breathing was the last thing he wanted to hear, he ran his palms along the walls, hoped and hoped for the exit that was there.

The Monk's Couch For Two

The monk gave up women and married god. Then he gave up god and married a bottle. The bottle was dull green, round on the sides like a store bought cookie, and flat, flat, flat on the bottom. The bottle made him laugh more than women or god ever did. At night, the monk would sit on one side of the couch and rub his feet and paint his nails. The bottle would sit on the other side and pretend to watch television. The monk liked sumo wrestling and home improvement shows. He would talk about all the places he wished to visit. As he got older, he learned of new places so his list became very long.

The Sensible Mathematician

All day he's thought of number 8...the endlessness of her circles...lusty squiggles that hint at infinity. He's tried other numbers. The loneliness of one. The trusty stool of three. Both disappointed with their jagged edges. He wants the fullness she contains. There's so much muchness there. He wants to swim and swim in her two lakes.

His Bubblegum

None of his bubblegum went to college. The old pieces
hung beneath his desk, his coffee table, his bed frame, and
his bathroom sink. When he wasn't around, they talked
and often described little glimpses of what they had seen.
A few had been to the movies. Several had gone on walks
to the laundromat and the park. One or two could warn
about accidents that can happen during a poorly timed
kiss. Mostly, they knew about spit, onions, and garlic.
None had seen enough to make a map larger than a hand.

Plane Ride Away

for John Gallaher

It was a red door called Georgia, hung on gold-painted hinges. Most days it stayed locked to mystery and whatnot. Some days, though, someone left it open. You should've seen all the riffraff going in and out! Parties lasted, long as sunlight and darkness. People hung all over Georgia, tried to rub the red off. Quite a few swore the hinges weren't painted, were actually 24 karat, and were so old they were hanging before Georgia was even a door.

Dream Without A Plot Or Title

Here we are again. You run naked down the sidewalk on a summer day. Every neighbor nonchalantly tosses a ball in his/her yard or else, that old standby, cuts grass. Embarrassed to be naked as sunlight. Then embarrassed no one notices. Not the mailman with his big blue bag of promises. Not the urbanized, moneyed couple who walk their alligator, pretend he loves them and his leash. Then there's your 10th grade math teacher. You haven't thought of the worn gap of her smile in years. She's there, on a front porch, dressed like the cat lady you always thought she was. With a smile and a wave, she tosses a loaf of French bread, shouts, *Keep running! This is all you need.*

Wounds

Every wound made him more invisible. One by one, they accumulated. Sometimes papercut small. Other times big as a toe, a foot, a leg. There was the divorce that cost him the house, the car, the cat, and a little more than half his heart. The job that called him too old and let him go and go. And the friend who took a trip past the end of the road. Each erased a little more. Until the morning when the bathroom mirror barely held a face to shave.

The Helpless Passenger

My luggage is in the trunk. For over an hour, the taxi driver hasn't answered any of my questions. He is arguing on the phone with his wife. She wants a new sofa because of the cat. He doesn't want a new sofa. The old sofa is fine for the two of them and fine for the cat. It's his cat and he should know what's best.

He is telling her in his most passionate and lyrical voice all of his many, many reasons for wanting to keep the old sofa. I'm sobbing quietly in the backseat over his words to his wife. He loves her. He loves the cat. He loves that damn sofa. The sofa is so, so lucky.

Traveler's Fable

A hotel, sick of ins and outs and noise complaints and made up stories at the hotel bar. Yes, a hotel sick of laundered sheets and room service and little scented soap bars and muffled one night stands. This hotel dreamed itself into a lunchbox, carried by a man at the mill. Opened and shut only a few times each day. There only for him. A thermos, the best company. The thermos once a lighthouse, years before.

The Tooth

Pull it, I tell the dentist.

He's dark-haired-handsome, spends lots of time at his
gym. His bright teeth the absolute opposite of black.

You'll have a gap on your left side, he says.

I'll fill it with gumballs transitioned to gum. Maybe implant
a tiny radio for jazzy tunes.
Fill it with my tongue when it wants to fill empty. Fill it
with words…all the Oxford ABC's. I'd fill it with a
rainbow, but it's dark in there. So, I'll fill it with quick
breathing instead. Along with a few sighs. I'll fill it with
wants near as now. Fill it with sometimes. Fill it with *in*,
out, and *of*. All things rightly needed. I'll open my mouth
and fill it with March's rainfall. Make a spectacle for
strangers and their kids.

I'll take the old tooth, build a castle. Decorate it with
peacock curtains. Pretend neighbors won't notice or, at
least, will understand.

My gap will have an alias. It won't be written down.

Runaway Ears

When I woke from my Sunday afternoon nap, my ears were gone. Both abandoned me without a note.

I checked the bathroom to see if they were cleaning themselves. I checked my phone to see if they were calling people, just to listen. I even checked the kitchen radio to see if they were spinning the dial higgledy-piggledy. (Though I unplugged the radio the week before for bi-annual cleaning.) They were not under rugs or in cabinets. They weren't in the coffee pot or on bookshelves.

Then, though my ears weren't attached, I heard wind among leaves.

I went outside and looked up among the trees. A hawk, all brown and lively, sat in the top branches of an oak with my ears in his beak.

Hey, hey, I cried.

He didn't look down. He just flew off.

Two weeks now and my ears still aren't back, though distant sounds never cease. Some days bells and cows. Some days passing trains. I hear rain and check for drops in my hair. Some nights the sound of cars muffling through an underpass lulls me into dreams

Her Loves

She loved corsets and dictionaries and various definitions of both. She liked to read her different dictionaries while wearing different corsets. She often did this while drinking herbal tea. She didn't really like tea, but was convinced of its goodness for her and her figure. No one could convince her otherwise. Even the medical librarian who came, daily, to brush sparks from the dark embers of her hair, and to charm with mouthfuls of polysyllables, even he could not.

Frank The Balloon Man

Honestly, he hated children. Hated their laughs and the miniature gaps of their smiles. Hated the clutching need of their fingers. He hated the parents. The ones who told their children what to say as if each was the conduit of a wish. And the ones who ignored their children, completely, as if each was a subject they never thought to master.

What he loved were the balloons. The feel of each in his hands, on his fingers. He loved the squeaks as he twisted shapes from intentions. And he loved the balloon animals. All of them. Each one fresh from an Eden, with a string leash that almost led back.

Folk Tale Without Neon Or Blessings

for Shawn Pavey

God was tired, so she took the day off. She was sick of panic and endless needs. Sick of that old scale of wants versus thanks. Couldn't fathom another roundabout day of angels gossiping over people whose magic scars they guessed at.

So, after yoga and a garden walk, she carved for hours on a rock she couldn't lift and studiously didn't think of kids. Late in the day, in dust white work clothes, with wind blowing just enough to lighten green on grass and leaves, she sat and sipped her tea and wondered how anything she ever made could still exist.

The Sundial

Scissors, sick of any line not completely straight, chased
Circle out of the house and locked the door. Circle,
though, knew how to make friends and quickly did.

All around Circle stones of similar size gathered, a dozen
in all, to hear of life inside the house and to hear of the
way all shapes came to be. Except on very dark, cloudy
days this became the routine.

Samson's Lion

When he came back to look at the bee-riddled carcass, it
was to mourn. After many months, parts of the desert
worn hide still shimmered. If the lion had not sprung
quickly off a shining rock, had not bared teeth and claws
with intention, he never would have struck. He loved most
animals more than most men.

The honey he found surprised him, by its place, its
abundance, by the sweetness the bees gathered and
gathered. He brushed aside the bees. Gave no notice to
stings. He sat in the dirt, amid sun and rock, dry bones and
honey. So filled with joy at the surprise of a desert feast, he
let honey drip from his mouth and beard.

Lot's Wife

The marriage was never good. Lot lived and lectured
within the dull walls of his piety. Never sipped water or ate
a crust of bread without giving thanks so all might hear. In
Sodom, his eyes watched the ground. When women stood
in doorways and called and called he did not answer.
Instead, he scurried down the one path to home. At night
his sand-coarse hands touched his wife: the same spots in
the same order. He knew only one way to enter the house
of her body...quickly, while shuddering thanks. Beneath
him, she dreamed of another's salt. Her whole life, a
backward glance.

She

Quotes old lovers as if they are references. Likes jesters better than kings. Asks to trade underwear, then argues about who best likes the trade. Goes around citing those Raymond Carver lines: *betrayal/ like bad credit/ begins with the fingers*. Then burns with her open palms. And places kindness in another purse. Though she carries magic wherever she goes. Knows potions are less potent than spells.

IV.

Recipe For Gold

- ❖ Burn a matchstick down to a thumbnail ember
- ❖ Crush the ember in an antique crucible, borrowed from a retired alchemist
- ❖ Add salt, but no more than a dove can carry on its smallest feather
- ❖ Toss in three red rose petals, moist with desire's blessings
- ❖ Wrap a black silk string, twice, around the crucible
- ❖ Close your eyes and sit with an unblended heart
- ❖ In all of this, never once think of dirt, water, or sky
- ❖ Results depend on soul purity, local miracle frequency

Easy Listening

I like to hum when I eat cake and when I smoke cigars.
Music and health are my main concerns. Cake is like
spinach salad, if you've never had spinach or salad. Cigars
are for people who like penis symbols hand rolled. If you
are a guy, everything starts or ends with the penis. Even
wars back to blind Homer on his rock. Especially those.
Peace never has a lasting start since history is a circular
clock. We can't tell time. So we are always early for the
next war. Every battle hymn, *tra la*, a little off key.

The Films Of Burt Reynolds

Not the films, but the book about the films. Yes, that's a
real thing. Someone loved Burt enough to watch each,
then write descriptively. Lots of cowboys and cops. Lots
of loners who stare back at remembered misdeeds. Lots
and lots of fast cars, one of which jumped a bridge into
movie timelessness. One appearance in a Woody Allen
movie. (The Woody Allen of the 1970's, everyone thought
edgy and fresh.) There's Burt with a mustache. Burt
without. There's Burt with one woman. Burt with two.
Burt young, though not very young. Burt middle-aged,
which seemed to last and last. Burt old, which happened in
a day and a half. When I was a boy and he was most
famous my mother said she'd marry him if he's just stop
by. Instead he walked down the red carpet with Dinah and
Lauren, Sally and Loni. Burt smiled at the camera. He had
a famous laugh.

People Who Should Have Been Hung By Their Boots, Like Mussolini

Idi Amin. James Buchanan. Henry Kissinger. My great-grandfather, Ted Wade. (A true, hateful bastard who was not loved by his family and is not missed.) Pol Pot. Pope John XII. Stalin. (Feel free to say of course to this one or any others.) Nathan Bedford Forrest. John C. Calhoun. Alexander H. Stephens. (Anyone who ever thought slavery a good idea.) Ivan the Terrible. Frank the Suspicious. Joey the Peevish. Leopold II of Belgium. Andrew Jackson. (Hung by his boots and painted Cherokee red.) Augusto Pinochet. (His deadly name always sounded like an umbrella being opened.) Not Jack Wolford, my late poet friend. And no women listed, since history's greatest forced errors are owned by men.

A Very Specific Curse

May grammar make a tight leash around you. Babel
descend on your tongue. Your dentures slip into whistles.
Those whistles your only music as you are called to dance,
dance. And you learn love can be flammable as you forget
every star you ever thought to touch.

Political Poem

There once was a man who knew almost nothing. He would have been fine left alone, growing old under a tropical sun. Unfortunately, the people asked him to be king. Most knew he knew nothing, though some knew less than him. (That's not mathematically possible, but is metaphorically true.)

People thought he would be like them and, in many ways, he was.

Whenever he travelled, which was often, he shook hands with almost anyone. When he shook hands he leaned in too close or stayed back too far or squeezed too tight or held on long past when he should have let go.

His mind, a blue blanket on the ground, held every shadow that came past. Shadows frightened him even more than stairs.

Alone in his castle, all he ate was ketchup and mushrooms. Ketchup was his favorite color and vegetable. After a while, after years of such a diet, the king died.

Before he was king, there had been many good years.

The Cheater

Cheated on his wife, yawn. Cheated on his boyfriend too.
Cheated D.B. Cooper out of his airplane money. Cheated
taxi drivers, which is nothing new. Cheated storytelling
strangers out of time. Cheated on his driver's license.
Cheated at the ballot, both voting and counting. Cheated
his lawyer, who was cheating his ex-wife. Cheated on IQ
tests. Cheated at tic-tac-toe, imagine that. Cheated at
ventriloquism, I've heard. Cheated the collection plate.
Cheated siblings out of inheritances...land and rugs and
hula skirts. Cheated death, more than once. Cheated at
speed reading. Cheated the blind pencil salesman. Cheated
Pol Pot, but kept that to himself. Cheated at sincerity and
mediocrity, too. Cheated his alarm clock. Cheated at being
a mime. Cheated at cards, which is nothing special.
Cheated other cheaters, which is. Cheated at drinking
contests with lots of water. Cheated on local, state, and
federal taxes. Cheated kids out of allowances. Cheated the
sky out of a rainbow. Cheated bubbles out of a bath.
Cheated the ocean out of the tide. Cheated the hook from
the fisherman. Cheated the fish.

The Prisoner

"One of the prisoners had not seen the stars for 22 years."
New York Times

That night, when he walked outside, he thought he was
living in memory. A boy, camping, the year before his
father died. No tent, but four blankets and a fire. The stars
all made of fire. Too far for night warmth. All of them at
the edge of where darkness starts and ends.

David Sees Bathsheba

The early evening brought nothing she needed. Shadowed softness hid no blemish from sun or eye. What was perfect under clear sky's brightness, remained at day's end. Bathsheba bathing knew only a hint of her beauty. Like the water of her bath, it was more than she could hold.

When David saw her, he saw her completely. Swore an oath to his one God. Felt her beauty as strong as a desert wind. So he wished to know her name and the breath that shaped it. Wished to hold all she could not. She would be the one lamb he would feast on, again and again, even when his hunger was filled.

V.

Michael Benedikt's Suitcase

Michael Benedikt's suitcase of poems. His leather suitcase
of poems. Michael Benedikt's off-white, leather suitcase
of poems. His crinkled, off-white, leather suitcase
of poems. Michael Benedikt's dumpster-bound suitcase.
A suitcase of poems, number two pencils, and paper clips.
No magazine cut-outs of air-brushed gloss within Michael
Benedikt's crinkled, off-white, ketchup-stained, leather
suitcase. The one with the gray trim. A suitcase not out-of-
place on a riverbank, engulfed in green grass and in the
green daydreams of lawyerly voyeurs. A suitcase that stays
full after a whole day and night and day of unpacking.

Variation on *The Outdoors Survival Manual*

When all else fails, you can always "pitch a tent" at an old circus camp. (That certainly sounds like fun.) There aren't too many circuses around these days so the old camps should be empty. Once you settle in, look for a trough full of big red shoes. The best might be unscuffed, barely worn. Those won't take the place of firewood. Only firewood takes the place of firewood. Those shoes will just keep you busy for a while.

Naïve List of Demands

So, look…the sun follows the same boring path since
before your grandma or country came along. Let it rise in
the west for a change. (Copernicus and his science be
damned!) Let's adjust, on a now and then basis, the hours
in the day. Encourage backwards walking throughout the
month. Along the way, allow trained snipers to teach
courses on politeness and grammar. Every police officer
should wear a blue, green, red, yellow, pink, purple,
orange, black, gray, white, or brown clown nose. That
might cut down on violent crime while teaching children
colors past the rainbow. And do something about
rainbows. There's no need for them to wait until after rain
comes around.

The Lottery Ticket In The Mail

for Scott Wannberg

Wasn't a winner. No one likes me that much. No return
address on the envelope. The ticket purchased the year of
my birth. Someone's sending a message I can't guess.

I'll put it on the refrigerator right beside the love notes
from Noam Chomsky, the death threats from each of the
last three popes, and the apple pie recipe my mother sent
right before she disinherited me and married a margarita.
My refrigerator door is a collage of disappointments. If I
ever opened it, I might sob into a river I couldn't cross.

I've given up keeping flowers in the kitchen. It's no fun
being a fan of anything that quickly dies. Just ask the man
who keeps fruit flies as pets. He spends half of each day
weeping.

That Last River

The Ferryman's patience is as endless as his river. And
though his task is simple, he must be paid. But not, slowly,
in pennies. And not in the paper currency of extinct
countries (i.e., Czechoslovakia or Central African Empire.)
And, before you ask, no, you cannot fish from his boat.
And you cannot take a turn steering. And you certainly
must not look back and wave to those on the disappearing
shore while shouting, "See you soon!"

Is & Not

There are so many things Mike is not. Like not especially
tall. Like that. More things he is not than things he is. Not
black, brown, or tan. Not female, though possessed of feet
and hands quite feminine. Not anyone other than a person
named Mike. No nicknames. No aliases. Someone who
often speaks in couplets and says *fuck* a lot. Who says fuck
more than he does fuck, which is the most people way.
Those named Mike. Those named Larry. Those named
Leslie. Those named Heather. Those who read Edward
Dahlberg with one eye shut. Those who file away old
postcards as if memory is an unchanging place. People
awash in prepositions *of, for, despite, without.*

About the Author

Mike James has been widely published in magazines, large and small, throughout the country. His thirteen poetry collections include: *First-Hand Accounts from Made-Up Places* (Stubborn Mule), *Crows in the Jukebox* (Bottom Dog), *My Favorite Houseguest* (FutureCycle), and *Peddler's Blues* (Main Street Rag.) He has served as an associate editor for the *Kentucky Review* and Autumn House Press, as well as the publisher of the now defunct Yellow Pepper Press. He makes his home outside Nashville, Tennessee. More information can be found on his website at mikejamespoetry.com.

www.ingramcontent.com/pod-product-compliance
Lightning Source LLC
Chambersburg PA
CBHW030154070426
42447CB00032B/1181